THE SMART KID'S GUIDE TO

Divorce

BY CHRISTINE PETERSEN • ILLUSTRATED BY RONNIE ROONEY

The Child's World®

Published by The Child's World®
1980 Lookout Drive • Mankato, MN 56003-1705
800-599-READ • www.childsworld.com

Acknowledgments
The Child's World®: Mary Berendes, Publishing Director
Content Adviser: Philip C. Rodkin, Professor of Child
Development, Departments of Educational Psychology and
Psychology, University of Illinois
The Design Lab: Design
Red Line Editorial: Editorial Direction
Amnet: Production

Photographs © Shutterstock Images, cover, 1, 6, 7, 9, 12,
15, 18, 20, 25, 28; Iakov Filimonov/Shutterstock Images, 8;
iStockphoto/Thinkstock, 11, 19; David Pereiras/Shutterstock
Images, 13; Thinkstock, 14, 17, 26, 27; Paul Vasarhelyi/
Shutterstock Images, 22; Darrin Henry/Shutterstock Images, 23

ISBN 9781626873407
LCCN 2014930677

Printed in the United States of America
Mankato, MN
July, 2014
PA02224

ABOUT THE AUTHOR

Before becoming a freelance writer, Christine Petersen enjoyed diverse careers as a biologist and middle school science teacher. She has published more than 50 books for young people, covering topics in science, social studies, and health. Christine is a member of the Society of Children's Book Writers and Illustrators.

ABOUT THE ILLUSTRATOR

Ronnie Rooney took art classes constantly as a child. She was always drawing and painting at her mom's kitchen table. She got her BFA in painting from the University of Massachusetts at Amherst and her MFA in illustration from the Savannah College of Art and Design in Savannah, Georgia. Ronnie lives on a U.S. Army base with her infantryman husband and two small children. Ronnie hopes to pass on her love of art and sports to her kids.

CONTENTS

CHAPTER 1

Happily Ever After? 4

CHAPTER 2

Different Directions 10

CHAPTER 3

Change, Change, Change 16

CHAPTER 4

Survival Guide 24

Top Ten Things to Know *30*

Glossary *31*

Books, Web Sites, Index *32*

CHAPTER 1
Happily Ever After?

Once upon a time, a beautiful young woman met a handsome prince. The prince asked her to marry him. Fireworks burst in the sky during their wedding. The royal couple rode home in a carriage pulled by two white horses. People cheered and waved as they passed.

This sounds like a fairy tale, but it really happened. Charles, Prince of Wales, married Lady Diana Spencer in 1981. Hundreds of thousands of people crowded onto the streets of London, England, on their wedding day. Another 750 million watched on televisions around the world.

Charles and Diana had a comfortable life and two beautiful sons. They seemed like the perfect family. So it surprised most people when the couple separated in 1993. Charles and Diana decided to live in different houses. Separation is like a break for married people. Some couples solve their problems during a separation. They move back in together later and stay married. This did not work for Charles and Diana. Instead, they chose to **divorce**. Divorce is a legal separation that ends a marriage. Charles and Diana had to work out **custody** for their sons. The boys lived part of the time with each parent.

Working together can strengthen relationships.

Adults usually marry because they love each
other and enjoy spending time together. They don't
expect to get divorced. But it takes more than love
to make a marriage work. Couples must **cooperate**
to care for a home and family. After marrying, some
people discover that they do not solve problems the
same way. This can lead to arguments and hurt
feelings. Or one **partner** may take a new job or go
back to school. Changes or new **stress** can strain a
marriage. Marriage is also hard if the couple does

not spend much time together. Sometimes the reasons for divorce are not so clear. People often change over the years. They become interested in new things. The partners no longer feel close or have much to talk about.

Big changes can strain a marriage.

Have your parents told you they are getting a divorce?

Do you have a friend whose parents are separated, divorcing, or breaking up? Maybe your parents divorced or have told you they plan to do so. If so, here are some things to remember. It is okay to feel worried, sad, or even angry. But you do not need to feel **guilty**. You did not cause your parents' divorce. Adults divorce each other because they cannot work out their own problems. You did nothing wrong.

Divorce brings change that you probably did not expect or want. It can take time to feel like things are back in balance. But your parents will always be your parents. You are still part of a family.

Do your parents argue a lot? This does not mean for sure that they will get a divorce. Some couples argue but don't stay angry. Tell your parents if you are worried about their arguing. They might not realize that it bothers you. You can also write in a journal to get out your feelings.

CHAPTER 2

Different Directions

The word *divorce* comes from an ancient language called Latin. It means "to turn in different directions." Parents divorce each other, not their children. But this change affects the whole family. Children can feel that they are being pulled in many directions. Everyone needs time to understand what has happened. They need to get used to a new way of life.

Moving is one of the first changes that comes with divorce. A family has many belongings, from dishes to cars. All these things must be divided up. In most cases, one parent moves out of the family home. Sometimes both parents have to move. Children are not belongings. But parents usually want to share time with their kids. Each family makes a different plan for custody. You might go back and forth between both homes. Some kids live with one parent most of the time. They visit the other on weekends, vacations, or holidays.

Even if you feel pulled in two directions, your parents' divorce is not your fault.

Changing schools is an opportunity to make new friends.

Parents sometimes move to new neighborhoods or towns after a divorce. It is okay to ask how those changes might affect you. Will you go to a new school? Maybe you can tour that school and meet your teacher before moving day. Is the new home close enough that you can still see old friends? If not, get your friends' addresses and phone numbers. Staying in touch will make the move easier. A new place may feel strange at first. Get out and **explore**! Find parks, movie theaters, and other fun places.

Are you nervous about meeting other children? Try to smile and say hello. You won't always be the new kid.

You might notice that your parents are busier after the divorce. Here is one reason why. Married couples usually take care of their home together. But most divorced parents must do everything alone. That includes cooking, cleaning, and shopping. They must also do chores like laundry and yard work. Most single parents also have jobs outside the home. Parents want to have fun with you! They may just

Both your parents will likely have more work to do after a divorce.

*You might hope your parents will get back together,
but you can't make them do so.*

feel too tired. You can offer to help. Chores get done
faster when everyone pitches in. Then you can invite
your parent to spend special time with you.

Some kids believe the divorce happened because
they were naughty. They work hard to be good
and stay out of trouble. But their actions—good or
bad—are not really why their parents divorced. And
their actions aren't likely to get their parents back
together, either. Many children want their parents to
get back together. It is natural to wish that a divorce

would go away. Maybe you feel your parents should stay together for you. The hard part is that adults divorce because of their own problems. You cannot fix them. But you can keep loving your family even after it has changed.

Some kids feel **relieved** when their parents separate or divorce. This is totally normal. It is tough for everyone if parents argue a lot or don't get along in other ways. Living apart can make parents happier and more relaxed. You can enjoy each other more. This is one of the positive changes that can come from a divorce.

CHAPTER 3

Change, Change, Change

People once believed that divorce was always wrong.
Couples were supposed to stay together for life.
It did not matter if they faced difficult problems.

But divorce is now legal in almost every country. You probably have at least one friend or family member whose parents are divorced. The fact that it is more common now does not make divorce easy. But more people now understand some of the changes and feelings that go along with it.

One or both of the parents will move after a divorce. It is not always possible for children to spend equal time at both homes. Sometimes parents make decisions about custody. But sometimes they ask

Even after divorcing, some parents still do not get along.

children where they would like to live. That's such a big choice. Children often worry about hurting one parent's feelings. It is okay to tell your parents that you can't choose. But don't be afraid to share your wishes. A judge can help, too. Judges work with families to make sure that divorce and custody plans are fair.

Some parents are friendly to each other after a divorce. Others still feel angry for a while. These parents might avoid talking. They sometimes ask

A judge might help your family make plans for the divorce.

their children questions about each other's lives.
Parents can even make the mistake of saying bad
things about each other in front of their kids.
They are upset. They might not see how this
affects you. But divorced parents must learn to
cooperate. They need to work together to take care
of their children.

Share your feelings with someone if you feel stuck
in the middle. Tell your parents if you can. If not,
talk to another trusted adult. This could be another

Speak up if you are feeling stuck between your parents.

relative, a teacher or counselor, a clergy member, or a family friend.

Divorce is a big change. Change is a difficult but natural part of life. You can learn to deal with it. But you may feel all mixed up for a while. Everyone in your family is going through the same thing. This process is called **grieving**. It is the great sadness that

It is okay to feel sad for a while.

comes after a loss. Grieving is different for everyone. Sometimes you feel sad. You don't want to do much. Your heart feels heavy in your chest. At other times, you might be angry or worried. Are you having bad dreams or skipping meals? Those are some other signs of grieving.

Your parents' divorce might seem like a reason to stop paying attention in school. Maybe you don't think it matters if you do chores at home, either. Sometimes you might even feel like yelling at people.

Have you ever shaken a closed bottle of soda? The drink sprays and bubbles out when you pop open the lid. Grief can be a lot like that soda. It's risky to keep it bottled up inside. The pressure might cause you to explode. Instead, talk about your feelings with a friend or loved one. Or write or draw about your feelings in a journal. Spend time with friends, too. Friends can help you feel less lonely when everything else is changing.

Try to enjoy the things you usually love doing.

Everyone understands that you are sad. But grief is not a good excuse for behaving badly. Let simple and normal activities keep you on track as your life changes.

Be sure to get some exercise! Moving can help you work through your feelings. There will be times when you feel okay. So, go have some fun! Laughter and friendship give you strength to make it through hard times. It is okay to cry, too. All these things help your heart heal.

Brothers and sisters are not always best friends. But getting closer to your **siblings** is another positive change that can come from divorce. Try to make peace with your siblings if you fight a lot. Your kindness will make things easier for younger brothers and sisters. Older siblings can help you get through changing times.

CHAPTER 4
Survival Guide

When divorce happens in your family, you might feel helpless. But you can do things to make the change easier. Think of this as your survival guide.

Living in two homes. If you live in two homes, you might often carry things back and forth. Your school backpack must go everywhere with you. You might have supplies for a sport or club, too. Kids sometimes carry their clothes in a suitcase or duffel. But it can be hard to feel at home if you have to pack your stuff up all the time. Maybe one of your parents has a small house or apartment. There might not be space for you to have your own bedroom. Still, your parent can probably find a drawer or basket just for you. Store clothes and favorite items there. A few books and toys can help you to feel more settled.

Ask your parents for two toothbrushes and similar items so you don't have to bring them back and forth.

Ask both your parents to check your calendar.

*Staying **organized**.* It helps to set up a calendar at each home. Adults should keep track of appointments, school events, and family activities. You can add things like playdates, parties, and games. It is important that your parents talk to each other about your schedule. Check the calendar often so you know what is coming up.

Keeping in touch. Living in two homes has ups and downs. You might get more time alone with each parent. That can be fun and healing for both of you.

But you might worry about the parent you are away from. There are many ways for you to stay in touch. Call on the phone, write a letter, send an e-mail, or video chat.

It's okay to miss one parent when you're with the other.

It's okay if it takes some time to get used to new family members.

New families. Your parents' lives will change after the divorce. Their new lives might include dating. It can feel weird to see your parents dating other people. You do not have to pretend you are happy if that isn't how you feel. It helps to be nice, though.

Sometimes a parent decides to marry again. That new partner becomes your stepparent. He or she might already have children. Those kids become part of your family, too. Life will change again if you have a stepfamily. Remember that having a bigger family does not mean your parents love you less.

There is an old saying: "Time heals all wounds." It does not mean that you will forget about the divorce. But at some point, you won't notice the hurt as much. You will build a new life that is good in different ways.

At times, you might envy friends whose parents are still married. But that doesn't make their families better than yours. Grab a piece of paper. Make a list of the things you love most about your life and the people in it. There are little and big things that make every family special, even after a divorce.

TOP TEN THINGS TO KNOW

1. It's okay to tell people about your parents' divorce. Lots of other kids have gone through the same thing.
2. There are healthy ways to let out your feelings.
3. Your parents should cooperate to take care of you. Tell them if you feel stuck in the middle of them. Or talk to another trusted adult about your feelings.
4. Being organized can help you deal with living in two homes.
5. It's okay to take some time to get used to the changes in your family and your life.
6. Ask questions to better understand how the divorce will affect you.
7. Hanging out with friends will help you feel less lonely.
8. It helps to stay in touch with parents when you are apart.
9. Enjoy the time you have with your parents, even if it is different than when they lived together.
10. Keep a good attitude! A divorce is hard, but it can bring positive changes to you and your family's life.

GLOSSARY

cooperate (koh-AH-puh-rate) To cooperate is to work together. Cooperate with your family members.

custody (KUHS-tuh-dee) Custody is the right to take care of a child. In a divorce, families must make decisions about custody.

divorce (di-VORS) A divorce is the official ending of a marriage. Many people move after they get a divorce.

explore (ik-SPLOR) To explore is to travel and discover new things. Be sure to explore your new neighborhood.

grieving (GREE-ving) Grieving is feeling sadness after a great loss. A time of grieving can last for a while.

guilty (GIL-tee) Feeling guilty is feeling ashamed or to blame for something. You should not feel guilty if your parents divorce.

organized (OR-guh-nized) Things that are organized are put together neatly or well planned. Try to stay organized during a move.

partner (PART-nur) A partner is either of two people in a couple. One partner changing can lead to a divorce.

relieved (ri-LEEVD) To feel relieved is to feel better about something. You might feel relieved after your parents divorce.

siblings (SIB-lings) Siblings are brothers and sisters. Sometimes siblings grow closer after a divorce.

stress (STRES) Stress is the state of being tense or uptight caused from being upset. Feeling too much stress might make you unhappy.

BOOKS

Kuklin, Susan. *Families.* New York: Hyperion Books for Children, 2006.

Murphy, Patricia J. *Divorce and Separation.* Chicago: Heinemann Library, 2008.

Wolfelt, Alan D., and Raelynn Maloney. *Healing after Divorce: 100 Practical Ideas for Kids.* Fort Collins, CO: Companion Press, 2011.

WEB SITES

Visit our Web site for links about divorce:
childsworld.com/links

Note to Parents, Teachers, and Librarians:
We routinely verify our Web links to make sure they are safe and active sites. So encourage your readers to check them out!

INDEX

arguing, 6, 9, 15

Charles, Prince of Wales, 5
children, 10, 11, 13, 14, 17, 18, 19, 28
custody, 5, 11, 17, 18

feelings, 6, 8, 9, 15, 17, 19–22, 24, 28

grieving, 20–22

homes, 11, 12, 17, 24–25, 26

judges, 18

keeping in touch, 12, 26–27

moving, 10–11, 12, 17, 22

organization, 26

remarriage, 28–29

school, 12, 21, 24, 26
separation, 5, 8, 15
siblings, 23
Spencer, Diana, 5